101 WAYS TO EVANGELIZE

Ideas for Helping Fearless, Fearful, and Flummoxed Catholics Share the Good News of Jesus Christ

SUSAN WINDLEY-DAOUST

GRACEWATCH MEDIA
WINONA, MINNESOTA
GRACEWATCH.ORG

101 Ways to Evangelize:
Ideas for Helping Fearless, Fearful, and Flummoxed Catholics
Share the Good News of Jesus Christ

Copyright ©2020 by Susan Windley-Daoust. All rights reserved. No part of this book may be reproduced by any means without the written permission of the publisher.

Permission is granted to individuals who have purchased this book to photocopy or duplicate pages for personal or family use. All other reprint requests may be directed to the publisher.
Contact us at info@gracewatch.org.

Printed in the United States of America.

Editing by Jerry Windley-Daoust.
Copy edited by Karen Lynn Carter.
Book design by Jerry Windley-Daoust.

Cover art: "Figure of Christ" by Heinrich Hofmann.

First Edition: 2020
ISBN 978-1-944008-65-9

GRACEWATCH MEDIA
WINONA, MINNESOTA
GRACEWATCH.ORG

PREFACE: "BE NOT AFRAID"

Evangelization is a scary word to lots of Catholics. For too many of us, our first thought is of the guy on a soapbox on the street corner screaming obscure Scripture passages interspersed with "YOU'RE GOING TO HELL." Or maybe you recall the couple going door to door for Religion X who just wouldn't leave. Or maybe you think of televangelists promising everything, delivering nothing, while rolling in money. No wonder Catholics run the other way when they hear the word evangelization! But it is long past time to set the record straight: evangelization is a good word.

Evangelization is simply sharing the message of Jesus Christ, the goodness of God in a world desperately in need of it. It's not imposing ... it's sharing great news! Traditionally, it has meant sharing the message of Christ with those who have not heard it before. We have many books full of stories of Christians evangelizing in foreign lands, finding ways to articulate the good news in very different cultures. These stories are fascinating, inspiring, but perhaps feel "far away." The shift we Americans need to make is that today, we live in a land increasingly foreign to the Christian message. More and more people (especially younger generations) identify themselves as having no religious affiliation, or as one of the "nones."[1] The secularity of our culture is increasingly one absent of religion. And let's be honest—in certain circles, there is hostility toward what people think is Christianity. Because God language is dropping from our public secular discourse[2] (and, when people do hear the name of God, it is muttered in vain or hostility), people don't look to the Church as a place of hope. People who are hurting or who have honest questions about God are simply not coming to us.

In addition to that, Pope John Paul II noted that we live in an age in need of a "new evangelization"—spreading the heart of the Christian message, the basic proclamation that God has a plan for each of us centered in Jesus Christ—to people who are already Christians. Many of us have fallen into a cultural Christianity, a comfortable social identity group that joins together for worship and practice but has not been challenged to open itself to the depth of the good news. Perhaps we attend Mass regularly or semi-regularly, but are more influenced on a day-to-day basis by a God-absent culture. By definition, we drift from where we should be without knowing it. We look into our hearts and know that drift is too easy. We all need to return to the reason for our hope, the core message of Jesus Christ.

The need is real. The news is GOOD. So why don't we dedicate some time to deliberately sharing the message that Jesus Christ has come for me and you, and allowing his grace in our lives to transform us in ways we never imagined?

But Aren't We Doing That Already?

In most cases, no. If we were, we wouldn't be losing people by double-digit percentages.

I know we're not standing still—parishes tend to be very active and engaged in vital community-building, catechesis, and service activities. But that work is not direct evangelization. We do a lot of insider discussion with those already Christian, presuming they don't need to be reminded of the story of our salvation. We do a lot of service for all people, regardless of their faith affiliation. And we enjoy each other, and have fun together. These are all good. But this booklet is focusing on one piece that is usually missing: direct evangelization—getting the core message of Jesus out there to people who need to hear it. This one missing thing is essential and roots everything else.

If you are now thoroughly confused, have no fear. It's time to define our key term via the *Catechism*: Evangelization is the proclamation of Christ by word and the testimony of life.[3] Evangelization always involves what is called the *kerygma*, or, if you prefer English, the *proclamation* Jesus and his disciples offer us. What is the kerygma, exactly? Basically, it has four steps:

1. **Good news!** Our all-powerful, all-good God, our Father, created the universe from nothing: and it was good. He created human beings as entirely good, and placed us in loving harmony with himself and the world.

2. **Bad news.** The first humans broke those perfect and good relationships by rejecting God, wanting to be our own gods. That first devastating sin broke the relationship between God and humanity, and that brokenness is part of our inheritance as humans. Now we are inclined to desire wrong rather than right, and evil exists.

3. **Good news!** The Father sent his Son, Jesus Christ, into the world—fully human and fully God—to teach the way, to love the lost, to preach repentance, to heal those in need, to raise others from the dead, and, ultimately, to sacrifice his life to create for us a path to union with the Father. Jesus died, and after three days, the Father raised him from the dead. He was seen, touched, and heard. He is alive! And he continues to give us himself.

4. **More good news!** Jesus Christ sent us the Holy Spirit to give us power, peace, and consolation to grow closer to Christ and to the Father, and to share the good news of God that life can be different, whole, better, and amazing.

Do you have to memorize all that? Well, no. *But you begin to see what evangelization is about: presenting Jesus as the Christ who saves and leads us to a life of everlasting peace and joy.* Sometimes you do get the opportunity to share the whole story. But usually you are offering the real hope of Jesus Christ to people in a specific situation, and the kerygma is more pointed—Jesus Christ has come for YOU, right here, right now. He is the source of healing and hope. You can trust him. God has a plan for you.

This is what we mean when we say Jesus Christ is the cornerstone, or the foundation. The Church exists to evangelize,[4] and we cannot evangelize outside of that relationship with Jesus Christ. Evangelization is less taught and more shared.

Don't I Need to Know Someone Well First?

Ideally, yes, you share the Gospel within relationships. Parishes should have deliberate pre-evangelization work (creating bridges of outreach, trust, and friendship) in place. But you know what? Paul, Peter, Silas, Philip, Barnabas, and others in the Acts of the Apostles presented the Gospel to people they did not know. Sometimes the Holy Spirit paves the way, and we step into that path. But even then: be sensitive. Sharing the good news works best when it is invited by the one being evangelized in some sense, such as when the person asks a question or demonstrates clear openness to conversation. Respect the person you are evangelizing, and, if they walk away or demonstrate clearly they want to stop the conversation, yield gracefully. God pursues each one of us in myriad ways. Perhaps another person is meant to share the Gospel with them, or perhaps they need to hear it more than once.

I'm Afraid.

There is a reason Jesus Christ continually said, "Don't be afraid." He knows our fear. This is one reason he promised us his Holy Spirit, and it was given to us at Pentecost and in our baptism. We are temples of the Holy Spirit! No one can say "Jesus is Lord" except through the power of the Holy Spirit. The Holy Spirit can counter our fear and give us the words that we need.

There is a reason that some of the most powerful evangelizers say they have been baptized in the Holy Spirit. Baptism, in this case, simply means immersion—but "simply being immersed in the Holy Spirit" is an amazing thing! Whatever language you use, deliberate openness to the work of the Holy Spirit, and praying for his grace, is key to pushing out fear.

But this booklet is meant to assuage any fears as well. Evangelization is doable, exciting, a joy, and can change another person's life. If you are intrigued, even chomping at the bit, but you don't know how to begin—this book is for you.

Anything given to God is not wasted. Don't fear failure. Fear not trying. If you put on Christ's love and share, you will be doing exactly what God desires, and he will work with it in ways that you may or may not see immediately. Wherever you go, God is already there, waiting for you.

How Do I Use This Book?

This book is meant for pastors, parish staff, and lay people. Some of these ideas are best implemented in groups and by a parish, but the idea is likely to be proposed by a layperson with the skill and desire to pull it off. Other ideas can be employed by individuals right away. If some of these are not for you, that's fine. No one can do all of them!

Pray, read, and keep an open mind. Some of these items are self-explanatory and need little discussion, so we move on. Some do require explanation. Perhaps you should consider this book a step into a brainstorming session. Not everything will be appropriate to your parish or to you personally, but some things will. They may inspire new ideas … write them down before you second guess yourself![5]

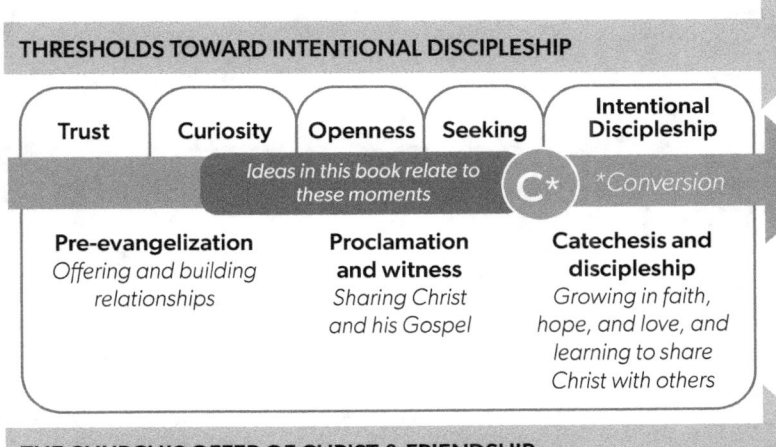

Remember, if you begin actively evangelizing, you need a plan for how to follow up. The image above[6] may give you a better idea of where evangelization "fits" in the life of discipleship, for the one being evangelized and the parish that is evangelizing: it typically begins with trust-building (friendship-based outreach) and ends with intentional relationship with Jesus and other disciples for growth.

Catechesis and discipleship, for example, may look like RCIA catechumenate, Franciscan Outreach's Discipleship Quads, adult faith formation, or many other options not explored in this book. (You can find more about this developmental image at creativeevangelization.org.) But think about where to support the newly evangelized after they hear and embrace the first message.

And finally, if you choose one thing and decide to do it, and you consider your evangelization box "checked and done" regardless of whether it bears fruit or not—you're doing it wrong. We should be looking for every possible opportunity to introduce Jesus Christ to others. As baptized disciples, we have been entrusted to a life mission. Let's get started!

THE LIST: 101 WAYS TO EVANGELIZE

Preparing to Evangelize

"You pay God a compliment by asking great things of him."
—attributed to St. Teresa of Avila

These ways to evangelize are essential and the building blocks to everything else. You will benefit by preparing yourself or your team in this way:

1. **Expectant faith prayer.** Both a life of dedicated personal prayer and prayer before and during each action are utterly essential to evangelization. Remember that the Holy Spirit is the evangelizer, who simply works through us. We also recall that Jesus Christ told us to make disciples of all nations, and to be his witnesses through the power of the Holy Spirit. We know the Father wants to embrace every daughter and son, and welcome each person into his healing and love. Finally, we know that God is the one who turns human hearts, not us; we simply present the opportunity to our brothers and sisters. So pray with humility, with confidence in God's love, and with the expectation that God, the source of miracles, is at work: that is, pray out of an expectant faith. Use your own words, but here is an example:

   > Holy Spirit, I want you to act in my life. Help me be an instrument of your power, your peace, and your love. Help the people I meet to hear the good news and sense the presence of Christ. Help me know how to love others and to act in that love. Holy Spirit, bring me to today's "divine appointment." May the name of Jesus be known and loved. In his name I pray. Amen.

   In addition, when there is a major event or evangelization action, it is good to have people praying for those working that action. This presents a great opportunity to invite into participation those who cannot, for any reason, be in public (the ill, the elderly), and this is a great intention to give adorers at parishes with Eucharistic adoration.

2. **Learn the art of invitation.** Catholics in the United States have a habit of presuming that people wanting to know about Jesus Christ and the Catholic faith will come to us—see, there is our church, right there on the corner. But it should be obvious that they do not come to us on their own. Virtually everyone who has been in an RCIA process has been invited. Others may be interested, or have questions, but don't even know where to start. *We need to learn how to personally invite people to opportunities to encounter Jesus Christ.*

That requires both vulnerability and modeling. A parish that wants to share the message needs to empower its people by offering confidence to move through the vulnerability, along with a method and language that can be used. You really can't just tell them to go and invite people. They need to be shown how and then given support. If you are reading this on behalf of a parish, before you do any of the following actions, find a way to deliberately teach and practice invitation to life in God.

For example: this way of invitation is a little involved, but it has everything covered and yields powerful results.[7] Say you have a parish mission coming. You want to intentionally invite those outside the church. First, print postcard-sized invitations and place them in the pews. After communion—or before the Mass begins—announce this event, talk about how it will make a difference in people's lives, and invite everyone there. But then explain that the invitations are not for them—they are for someone else they know. Ask everyone to quietly consider: who do they wish knew more deeply the love of God? Ask them to pray for that person now, quietly. Then have them hold up the invitation cards while the priest or deacon blesses the cards. Finally, tell them: you have a mission this week. Give your card to that person and invite them, telling them that you thought of them when you heard of this event. Tell them they could come with you. You will be amazed how many show up.

3. **"Share your story" training.** Saint Paul Evangelization Institute has a great primer on how to share your faith story in 2–3 minutes.[8] Getting people together to try this with each other is great practice for sharing pieces of your story as needed. But at minimum, you want to be able to answer the question, "Why do you believe in Jesus Christ?" This is not about theology as much as it is about your life of faith, and how Jesus makes a difference in your everyday life. The doctrine is important, but, before that, most people want to know your story. They can get the doctrine on Wikipedia, or in a book. They can only get encouragement to take a chance on Jesus through you. You are their living evidence that Jesus matters. Practice answering that question, and, if you are in leadership in a parish, get others to do so as well.

Start with Low-Hanging Fruit

4. **Contact the "Missing in Action."** Go through your list of registered parishioners, note the ones you haven't seen for a while, and call for a "check in." (This is a valuable thing to do for your entire congregation, attending or not, spread out over the year.) Call and say that you're contacting every household in the parish to check on people, to see how they're doing, and to get a better sense of how we can be a community of disciples for each other and the world. After they stop sputtering in surprise, ask if they are available to talk right now, or if they would prefer to come and have coffee or tea sometime this week. At that point, you follow their lead. Some may hang up. Some may handle this in a perfunctory way. Others may open up or really want that coffee. In any case, be kind, listen. If they are belligerent, turn the other cheek and part ways in peace. Earn their trust so they might open up. Apologize if they have felt slighted or unseen in some way. If they want to debate Church teaching, try to move to an in-person coffee talk for dialogue rather than debate. However, if they are personally struggling or ambivalent to the faith, Fr. John Riccardo has shared what he says: he shares his own story as to how Jesus Christ has changed his life, and why he believes Jesus has a plan for you as well, loves you, and wants a relationship with you.[9] This doesn't ignore the need for other helps (medical, psychological,

more), but offers what we are called to offer: a path to Jesus Christ, who works with these natural supports.

5. **Contact the "Missing in Action," variation.** Don't just go down your registered households list. Ask parishioners to give you the names of people in town who used to be connected to the parish (many of these may be adult children). In this case, when you contact, state, "We miss you ... and we're not calling to scold, but want to be humble, listen, and learn why you aren't attending anymore. Was it something the church did, or did life get busy ...?"

> ### Seed Sowing vs. Ground Tilling
> All of the ideas that follow fall into one of two categories: seed sowing or ground tilling. As Jesus said in Matthew 13, the seed is sown liberally by the Farmer (that is God, through us). We are called to sow the saving Word in all kinds of ways. The people hearing the Word (receiving the seed) are the ground. That ground needs to be tilled! So sometimes, direct evangelization involves tilling the ground: helping the ground itself soften, giving it water, banishing the weeds in the way. Most direct evangelization involves both seed sowing and ground tilling, but some actions focus on one more than the other. Throw the seed, don't hold back, and remember that tilling the ground looks a lot like Christian friendship.

Out in "the Agora"

This section deals with bringing the proclamation and/or proposal of Jesus Christ as the answer in public gathering spaces. The "agora" was the open space where public gatherings occurred in ancient Greek city-states. What are your agoras?

6. **Performing the Gospel in the Park.** Does your city do Shakespeare in the Park? Then you know what I am talking about. Seriously—get your best theater folks and perform the Gospel of Mark in the park. Yes, you can even call it Mark in the Park. (Look for Max McLean's one-man

show on the Gospel of Mark[10] to give you an idea of how this could be done, although it could be reader's theater, the work of a troupe, etc.) Invite people to a Bible study on Mark that begins within the week.

The delightful part of this idea is that, as biblical scholar Richard Horsley holds, this is exactly how the Gospel of Mark (the earliest recorded Gospel) was likely shared: mostly all in one piece, "performed" in the marketplace.[11] People would stop, listen, and sit and stay for the whole message. You could be doing exactly as the disciples first did. The brave may be interested in doing it as actual "street theater." (If you do, have someone there handing out invitations to the church.) The key is getting excellent and committed thespians to put in the work to pull this off.

7. **... Or *Godspell*.** Musicals take a lot more effort, but the more involved means the more invested to invite those who haven't heard the Word. Ideally this would be in a public space where people can stop by (for example, a bandshell or an amphitheater), but it could be an auditorium if your invitation initiative is strong. It is still ideal to hold this in a place that is NOT the church or church-related school if you want people on the outside to feel comfortable and safe in coming.

8. **Weekly prayer in the park.** Do a prayer tradition that is unusual and beautiful so people will be intrigued by the unknown. Taizé requires good musicians, but is very easy for new people to join in. Or ... Gregorian chant with a relatively simple evening prayer? End the prayer with a simple message that God has a plan for your life ... and if any of you want prayer, please approach one of the people in the back or on the platform.

9. **Meditative prayer on the lake/river/beach.** Look, if people spend money to do yoga on flatboards on a lake, we can certainly offer prayer on the lake for free. The leader should be someone who can explain very simply what to do and who can make it meditative but Christ-centered. Advertise that all are welcome. But make it Christian meditation—harbor no confusion on that.

10. **Transform the parish festival into a street festival or park festival.** It may be more convenient to hold the annual parish festival in the church complex, but you'll get people outside your church to attend if it is elsewhere. This is especially effective if your church is linked with an ethnic group that uses that weekend to cook all the delicious food of the homeland! Same with traditional music. But whether the event takes place on church property or not, have a table present to offer prayers and provide information and welcome to the church itself.

11. **Summer concert series in the park.** Got musicians? Have a budget for musicians? Expose people to sacred music, gospel music, or any music that shares the message. Sponsor, or co-sponsor, a series in the local park. Have an interest table set up at the back. Invitation is key to this one.

12. **"Ask Catholics Anything" coffee hour at the local coffeehouse Saturday mornings.** This is the "Ask a Priest" phenomenon taken out into the marketplace—although it is set up with, yes, the pastor, but maybe with a couple of other Catholics too. The key to this is advertising and consistency.

13. **Praying in public.** Saint Paul Street Evangelization (part of Saint Paul Evangelization Institute, streetevangelization.com) does a phenomenal job teaching people how to do peaceful, nonconfrontational evangelization—with a lot of free rosaries and information, a dose of friendliness, compassion, listening, praying with people, and being a sign of hope. Check them out and do (or bring to town) their basic evangelization training, because the skills they teach serve in many places. Where? Streets, yes, but also:

14. **—In farmer's markets** (when they let you reserve a booth);

15. **—Outside stores** (with their permission—Walmart tends to be open to this);

16. **—At county and state fairs** (reserve a booth); and

17. **—At local festivals and sporting events** (at a booth or nearby on the sidewalk, which is legal, as long as you don't block foot traffic).

18. **Youth group evangelization.** SPSE also has a low-cost training specifically for youth groups. Young people, accompanied by their leaders, really have a special gift for this. People are often more comfortable approaching teens giving away rosaries and prayer pamphlets than adults. And when teens pray with sincere faith over adults? It's powerful, and can melt hearts.

19. **Praying with wait staff.** This is another Saint Paul Street Evangelization trick from regional missionary Deb McManimon. When you go out to eat in a restaurant and the server brings your order, say you are about to pray over the meal and ask if there is anything for which she needs prayers. Deb says people usually are surprised and touched, and mention something. Then, of course, pray. If the restaurant isn't busy, ask the server if she wants to stay for the prayer. If she seemed responsive to the prayer request, when she comes with the check, offer her a miraculous medal, small crucifix, or something, and offer that you think God wanted her to have that to remember that God has a plan for her life. Slip in the name of your church and that she is welcome, or leave a phone number if it seems that the person is open to talking more. And be sure to tip!

20. **Invite people to pray for the city in your church.** The last of the SPSE recommendations is based on an event they do in Detroit called "Light the Fire." One evening, they set up an inner-city church for prayer, light the candles, and have priests and others available for prayer in the corners of the church. Others working with SPSE comb the nearby streets and ask everyone they meet, "Hey, do you think Detroit needs a prayer?" Usually the response is, "You better believe it," to which they respond, "We want to invite you to go to the Church of ___ and pray for Detroit. We're praying for Detroit all night. Want to come? I'm going there now." People

often come, and the evangelist welcomes them into the church and explains: "You pray for Detroit in those pews there—God is right there (point to the tabernacle)—and if you have questions or simply want prayers for your own life, those people in the corners will help you out there. Thanks for caring about Detroit!" And the evangelist goes and gets more people to come. They have had up to 500 people come in off the streets to pray for Detroit in an evening, and many received personal prayer as well. This has been so successful that SPEI has found a way to adapt the event to other communities. See more here: streetevangelization.com/lightthefire.

21. Blessing of the running shoes at races/praying. Races are fun but focused events. Arranging a way to bless the shoes of the participants before the race is a great way to connect with people. You could do this before a race in a casual way (there is a lot of standing around before a race) by asking groups of people if they were interested, or by doing it for all the racers 30 minutes ahead of the start time. If it is a big race and people come in the night before, you could do it that evening, combined with a pre-race meal for racers. Work with people in your parish who are racing to see when the best time for this would be—racers are mentally prepping themselves before a race, so don't expect much interaction. But it is a great seed-sowing activity, and you can offer to be there to pray with people who get hurt, or who want prayer for any reason afterward.

22. Everyone loves a parade. Parades are about happiness and fun. Think of what a float would look like, centered on the proclamation. Singing (or blasting) praise and worship music? "Jesus Christ has a plan for your life, find out more at ___ Church." "Need prayer? Stop the float!"

23. Positive sidewalk chalking. Talk the talk, walk the walk, and chalk the walk! Get as many people in your parish as you can to chalk a positive message on their front walk. Give them a piece of chalk to do it. Focus on messages that make people smile, such as: Jesus loves you; Hope has a name— Jesus; Come seek God with us at ___

Church. Make it a challenge, and ask families to take a picture of the sidewalk and send it to the parish (to post them on the parish Facebook page!). Follow up with a letter to the editor explaining to people what they have seen, and inviting them to find out more at _____ Church.

24. Art festival/gallery: sacred art. Cathedrals often serve as a space for public sacred art, but you don't have to be a Cathedral to do this. Beauty is one of the three transcendentals, and it attracts one to God. Announce that you would like to create an art show that would draw people closer to God. The easiest theme would be "For the beauty of the earth," and encourage your photographers and artists of various media to offer works for show. It would be best to work with someone who is an artist on how to do this best: Juried? Strictly amateur? Have an opening with wine and cheese and Christian music in the background. Have people leave with a flyer about your parish. Again, invitation is key to this as an evangelization event.

25. Sand sculpture/ice sculpture/chalking the Word contest. This is a more humble iteration of the above. Choose a kerygmatic Scripture that should inspire the art, put it on a big banner, and give people a day to do the work. Open this to the public, make it festive, and encourage the artists in the community to come and support it. A winner's prize at the end would lure people in.

26. Iconography retreat. If you can secure someone who is an experienced iconographer to teach others how to do it, this could be a wonderful teaching/praying/evangelization moment for people who are artistic. Try to do this one on your property. Advertise in art circles, community education circles, etc. Make clear that it is open to anyone wanting to learn about this spiritual practice of art.

27. Create a film festival. You may be surprised to know how many young people are creating their own films with iPhones and such … currently, there is a huge interest in independent filmmaking and animation. Creating a film festival with films around a Christian theme (for example, mercy or hope or friendship) could be a great outreach. Include a couple of panel talks, one on the brass tacks of film creation (by people who know—Zoom them in if you have to), and one on the Christian message and the arts (St. John Paul II gives you a lot to work with). If your church has the appropriate space for this, great—but you may need to work with a school or even a movie theater, which may work to your advantage. If you have the equipment, a drive-in movie setup could work! Films could be from Grassroots Films, students at John Paul the Great University, Wild Goose Ministries, Holy Spirit Media, Fellowship for Performing Arts, and your own local submissions. Create a "teens session" of five-minute shorts. Advertising, invitation, and tone are key to making this a successful evangelization effort.

28. **Create a dance festival.** Similar to the above. Get people involved who are experienced in dance to help.

29. **Train people to witness inside the parish.** We've already mentioned St. Paul Street Evangelization as a great resource for training. Another possibility is Catholic Evangelization Outreach, which trains people to share their stories within the church, at evenings dedicated to sharing witness. This builds Christ-centered communities, makes it "normal" to talk about a relationship with Jesus, and gives people space to speak. You can find more about them here: crceo.info.

30. **Christmas caroling.** Christmas caroling is the easiest way to get people to evangelize. People are moved, they smile, and caroling is warmly welcomed. Make it evangelization by focusing on Christian hymns and handing out "You are welcome to come to our church for Christmas!" sheets. Obviously, you can do this in neighborhoods, especially the neighborhood surrounding the parish, as well as in:

31. **—Hospitals** (call ahead);

32. **—Assisted living/nursing homes** (call ahead); and

33. **—Jails and prisons** (don't skip this one, because most people do and it is deeply appreciated by prisoners).

34. Flash mobs (at Easter and Christmas especially). More choral evangelization! Go to the mall or a local store during the season and break into harmonized song. You'll find many examples on YouTube to inspire you. Be sure to end by inviting people to your church (simply ... afterword, all together, "We're from _____ and you are welcome to come to our church for more! Merry Christmas!")

35. Offering confession ... at the mall. If you have a couple of priests willing to hear confessions in public, reserve a space at the local indoor or outdoor mall with a sign, a couple of stand-up screens for some privacy, and a few people to explain what is going on and to create some privacy space. You may be VERY surprised at how many take advantage of this ... they seem to take it as a sign from God to confess NOW. Often these are people who have been away from the sacraments—and the Church—for years. Even if no one comes, people's curiosity will likely be piqued, which presents a good conversation point with people you don't know. Where else can you do this?

36. Music festival/sporting event confessions. Why not? If it is a public park or street you can do this! Or ...

37. Parking lot confessions. We've done this in front of the big box store with St. Paul Street Evangelization.

38. Bar/coffeehouse evangelization with Alpha/ChristLife. Alpha and ChristLife[12] are two similar presentations of the proclamation that focus on food and hospitality, on meeting people where they are, and on providing space for real conversation. They are both angled to present to those who know relatively little about Jesus Christ. Both are designed to be flexible in space and format, and, in an age of streaming video, can be taken almost anywhere. While many parishes run this on their property fruitfully, the ideal setting is in the community, outside of the parish. People who are curious are going to be more comfortable with a "neutral site." Check with a bar or coffeehouse for permission, but neutral sites could also include:

39. **—Home-based Alpha/ChristLife.** Invite some friends for grilling and good conversation.

40. **—Recreation centers, libraries, etc.** You will need to reserve or rent space.

41. **—Prison outreach.** You will need to get permission and work through the chaplain's office. This is best combined with concrete "nonspiritual" help to the prison as well. The fruit of this could be immense, but keep in mind that you are establishing relationships, and prepare to come back at least once a month for follow-up.

Offering Christ the Healer

The "good news/bad news/good news" method of the proclamation can really be summarized by offering Christ to people in their known brokenness. People in pain are looking for the Divine Physician. Healing is a way of speaking about salvation that most people understand more readily, and people who receive Christ's treatment for their pain are also more likely to become aware of their own sin and need for forgiveness. Offering Christ the Healer as a first move in evangelization is completely biblical and logical. How do you invest in that in your community?

42. **Healing outreaches: addiction.** There are many ways to approach this, but consider Catholic in Recovery (catholicinrecovery.com), which is based in a 12-step method but adds Catholic spirituality to the discipleship process. All are welcome.

43. **Healing outreaches: divorce and broken homes.** There is a great need for a deeper understanding of the Church's teaching about divorce, but it must be combined with the support for those going through divorce, for parents and their children. Consider a parenting night dedicated to blended family parenting or the parenting challenges of shared custody. There is a particular struggle and pain there not well understood by society, but Christ, through his Church, can help.

44. Healing outreaches: mental health. People are often afraid to address mental health so they "leave it to the professionals," but reaching out to the professionals to work in tandem with them would go a long way. Hosting Emotions Anonymous (a 12-step process for depression and emotional disorders), Depressed Anonymous, Catholic Charities depression/anxiety awareness evenings, and employing some of the inclusion markers for people living with mental illnesses (available from the National Alliance for Mental Illness—Faithnet [nami.org/Get-Involved/NAMI-FaithNet] are possibilities. For parishes that have parish nurses, how about providing monthly depression and anxiety checks?

45. Healing outreaches: abuse. This is hard but also necessary. If there is a person in the parish who is wise, spiritually grounded, and an abuse survivor, they could help establish an outreach … either by serving as a resource, sponsoring an event, or hosting a support group. Such outreaches must be backed or joined by psychological expertise. This is closely related to other outreaches discussed below.

46. Healing outreaches: #MeToo. I know many people think this is too hot to handle. Would Jesus have thought that? Dawn Eden Goldstein's *My Peace I Give You: Healing Sexual Wounds with the Help of the Saints*[13] is an excellent book on Catholic paths of healing through the lives of the saints. This is worthy of a book group; just see who shows up.

47. Healing outreaches: grief. Many churches have grief counseling groups, and this is a great good. Do we put the consolation of Christ at the center of them? Do we deliberately invite outsiders through hospitals, hospices, and other organizations?

48. Healing outreaches: abortion. The survivors of abortion, women and men, are often confused and crushed with guilt. An outreach based in compassion and healing could be very valuable. Invite a Sister of Life to come for a day of reflection, or perhaps you can invite some who have repented and continue to recover from abortion in your area. Prayer and blessing for those who are not Catholic can go a long way toward knowing the merciful healing of Christ.

49. Healing outreaches: Courage apostolate. If you are same-sex attracted, it is good to have a place in this culture to tell you that you matter and have value as a son or daughter of the Father before and during your orientation. It is also good to have a place where you find encouragement in your quest to live as a whole person without acting on that attraction, and where you can spiritually grow. Courage provides that. Perhaps no other place does right now.

50. Healing outreaches: Unbound prayer. Unbound, created by Heart of the Father Ministries,[14] is a deliverance prayer ministry that has led thousands of people to freedom in Jesus Christ. The prayer process, which involves a gentle interview, a leading of prayers of faith and forgiveness, and a renouncing of lies and/or evil spirits that ruled one's life, is a powerful healing prayer for those who have undergone trauma of any sort. Training a team at a local parish and advertising this prayer as available to all in the community is a genuine outreach.

51. Show, don't tell: healing service. Friends, if you have the confidence to invoke the power of healing prayer in public, or even to invite someone with that gift to offer an evening of healing prayer at your parish, this can be a powerful witness. As Damian Stayne says, when people are miraculously healed, they virtually always become committed disciples of the Lord.[15] You simply don't forget events like that. And when people see that happen, it is a powerful moment of decision. Jesus knew what he was doing when, before he taught a single thing, he ministered to the people by healing them.

Many people are hesitant to offer a healing service like this in their parish because they are worried about how this will affect people who are not healed there. It is right and true that everyone present should be healed in some way, and should leave knowing the love of God for them.

There must be an emphasis on Jesus as our spiritual healer at this service, a loving explanation of why some are not physically healed, and a commitment to follow up with whomever wishes for continued prayer ministry.

52. **The Gospel heals: send a group on a Cursillo retreat.** Most of these evangelization options are local, but it can be okay to support an out-of-town event. Cursillo retreats tend to be centered in large cities, and are powerful proclamations of the Gospel. They also create discipleship groups to meet locally after the retreat. What if your church not only encouraged parishioners to attend one, but also rented a bus and paid for part of the cost for people outside the church to attend?

Praying for Signs and Wonders in Public

The book of Acts is marked by how the original apostles proclaimed the Gospel with accompanying signs and wonders. Despite a 2,000-year difference, there is no reason that cannot happen now. But what would it look like? The following are listed in order of how much courage each takes.

53. **Praying with college students before exams.** Find out when the local college has midterms or exams, and set up a table (on campus with permission, or maybe on the sidewalk nearby). Hand out free rosaries, prayer cards, and medals, and also have a big sign that says "FREE PRAYER FOR EXAMS." (People are attracted to the word "free," but perhaps include a smaller line that clarifies that prayer is always free.) You can decide how to pray from there: a priest or deacon could give a blessing; a person could pray for best efforts on a particular exam, etc.

    But it will fall in the "signs and wonders" category if you pray in the name of Jesus for peace, and for the Holy Spirit to pour peace on that person. Ask before the prayer how anxious they are on a scale of 1 to 10. Offer the prayer, but tell them it will take two minutes (they may be rushing to class). Pray for the peace waterfall from Jesus Christ. After two minutes, ask again what their anxiety level is. I promise: 99% of the time it will be less. If it isn't, tell them it sometimes takes time to sink in, to wait for it, and then bless them on their way. Be sure to tell them where Jesus lives (your local parish) to experience more of that peace!

54. **Community service plus prayer.** These next two ideas come from Robby Dawkins' book *Do What Jesus Did*,[16] which is not theologically Catholic in places but he clearly is a devout disciple of Christ—and he has great ideas about how to do evangelization on the street. This is one of the best ideas: "clean souls, clean bathrooms." Take a youth group (or even adults) downtown with toilet cleaning supplies, a mop, and more. As a group, go to each business and tell the manager or owner that this group is from _____ Church, and we're giving back to the community today. We're going up and down this street washing people's bathrooms for free. Would you like us to wash your bathrooms? (Everyone says yes … and the kids with two adults go and clean bathrooms.) The leader stays up front and chats with the manager or owner, and asks if they would like a prayer for prospering and peace. They usually say yes. Offer that prayer in the name of Jesus, that Jesus Christ's peace will be made real to them right now. Be sure to ask them if there is anything else they need prayer for in their life outside of work, or if there is someone else they want to pray for. Go wherever the prayer takes you. This is powerful "good will" evangelization. Plus, clean bathrooms!

55. **"Power evangelization."**[17] This is a general process that employs Jesus's promises to send the gifts of the Holy Spirit (the "power") toward evangelization. It makes sense—Paul himself said the gifts of the Holy Spirit were for the edification of others, not ourselves—but it requires a certain comfort level with risk, as well as a sensitive life in the Spirit. This can include offering to pray for healing people on the street and employing a gift of prophecy for others' good. What does this look like? 1) Offer to pray with people. 2) Discern what needs prayer, and ask if that is true (or they may offer what in their life needs prayer). 3) Begin by praying, "Lord Jesus, I ask you make your presence real to _____ today so that he/she will know you are God, you love him/her, and you want a relationship with

him/her." If you sense it is appropriate, pray for that need to be healed in the name of Jesus. (Never pray anything that you sense is wrong, or that you cannot honestly say.)

Now, you will ask—what if nothing seems to happen? First, the prayer was for today ... tell them to be aware of how God may be reaching out to them today. Remember that God is always reaching out to us, all day long—this is no risky prayer! Second, regardless of how the prayer is received, end with "God loves you." Most people have never heard that said to them. It is powerful and healing in itself. Of course, encourage them to come to your parish to learn more!

Community Events Targeted to Maslow's Hierarchy of Needs

As Catholics, we tend to start at the deep end, putting the biggest faith questions first. And while that suits some people, it doesn't suit most who are ambivalent about the prospect of faith—and that is the world we live in. As St. Paul said, he first gave people milk, and then gave them meat (1 Cor 3:2). Abraham Maslow's hierarchy of needs, a psychological proposal of human motivation, may suggest that evangelization meets people best at their first and second needs. Consider creating community events that address those human security and psychological needs, proposing Jesus Christ as the root of the solution. Pairing a speaker coming from a spiritual perspective with a person coming from the other relevant perspective could help people remember that leaning on God does not mean ignoring the insights of the natural world that God created.

56. **Anxiety talk.** According to the NIHM, 21% of adults in the United States had an anxiety disorder diagnosis in the past year. The numbers for our youngest generation (teenagers) are skyrocketing, approximately 31%.[18] We don't want people to ignore their mental health care providers, but we do want people to know that Jesus is the Prince of Peace. A person can seek help from both medical professionals and the Lord, and usually should! Fr. Jacques Philippe's *Searching For and Maintaining Peace* is a relevant and helpful book.[19] Find the right speaker(s) to

offer a talk to the wider community. This is a public health crisis, but also a spiritual health crisis, and Jesus offers himself for both.

57. Bullying talk. This is another profoundly felt reality with our teens, but increasingly with our adults as well. This talk would have a deeper emphasis on human dignity. Look up the story and person of Lizzie Velásquez, a young Catholic woman with a rare disease that affects her appearance, who speaks on God's love, our identity in that love, and human dignity. Her witness, and the witness of others, serve as powerful proclamation.

58. Forgiveness talk. Virtually everyone on earth needs to forgive someone, but rarely do we tell them how. Events that are impossible to forgive become possible when we do it through the power of Jesus. Teaching forgiveness is natural evangelization work that introduces people to the power and gift of Jesus Christ.

59. Finances reordering. Learning to allow God, rather than money and debt, to rule your life is a powerful lesson, but it often requires help to get out of debt. What if you offered a talk called "Putting Money in Its Place" and discussed how we cannot let money be our Lord and Savior—we already have one named Jesus? Then you can follow up with either Financial Peace University (financialpeace.com), Compass Catholic Financial Ministries (compasscatholic.org), and/or social support through Catholic charities or local social services. FPU comes from an evangelical perspective, but it is Christian in orientation and an excellent tool for getting out of debt. However, the first talk is the evangelization moment—the follow-up helps people live out the call.

60. Parenting support. Parenting can be very hard. Offering a series of talk for parents on how to raise children well in our time could be of wide interest. Topics don't always need to be obviously religious, but encouraging a relationship with Jesus Christ could be part of any of these. Potential topics include dealing with social media, to cell phone or not to phone, fostering friendships, working against an achievement culture, kids and mental health, getting kids outside, the chore monster, raising compassionate kids, and raising nonmaterialistic kids.

61. **Adoption support.** This could be addressed in two ways: first, by raising awareness about fostering, children available for adoption, and how many orphans exist in the world (153 million, according to UNICEF);[20] and, second, by offering community support of adoptive parents before and after the adoption.

62. **Chronic illness support.** Dealing with a chronic illness is a challenge most on the outside do not understand. 40% of people in the US live with a chronic disease.[21] Now you know we need to reach out!

63. **Body image support.** This may seem atypical for a church, but people working on weight loss (or gain) and body image have a great deal to gain from seeing themselves as fearfully and wonderfully made, and as beloved sons and daughters of the Father.

64. **Respite day for peace, silence, and reflection.** This falls under the unstated Maslow need: "people just need a break." You need good space for this, but the idea is to create a respite time open to the community—easier to get to and engage in than a full blown retreat. If you have rooms or spaces set apart with a comfy chair for prayer, journaling, reading, etc., and offer a simple lunch, you can do this! Make it free if you possibly can and encourage attendees to take advantage of the opportunity to pray in the church. If people need to talk, make someone available. Have a few people praying offsite for the participants (and let them know that). Work with social agencies to advertise it as a respite day open to everyone.

65. **The "Purpose-Driven Life" talk (i.e., vocation).** We hear a lot of requests and prayers for religious vocations, but not witness talks. Offering these would kill three birds with one stone: creating a culture of witness; raising awareness about religious vocations; and directing focus to the reality that every human being receives a call from Jesus Christ. There is a reason Rick Warren sold

millions of copies of his book, *The Purpose-Driven Life*. People are, in the end, craving purpose. Purpose comes from encountering Christ.

66. **The need-sensitive parish mission.** (Look at how long it took to get to the idea of a parish mission!) Parish missions can be great opportunities for internal renewal. But they can have a deeper outreach if they are directed toward addressing one of these needs above, at least as a launching pad.

Specific Invitation and Welcome

A lot of these ideas are meant to take you to meet people outside the walls of your church, but I've also included a few ways to invite people into that space as well.

67. **Welcome weekend for those interested in how Catholics worship.** Consider dedicating a weekend to welcoming to Mass those people who are curious about the Catholic faith. Make it a "teaching Mass"—the priest can explain what is happening throughout (or provide a handout for everyone). Prepare people ahead to increase the hospitality (especially with hospitality ministers!). Prepare and teach parishioners to invite others to "come and see." Offer a Q and A session with donuts and coffee afterward, and provide an invitation to stay in touch.

    Keep in mind, if you do this, you will have to explain why Catholics reserve the reception of the Eucharist for those who have been initiated into the Catholic faith and are in a state of grace. However, a humble explanation that encourages everyone to pray for unity, along with the offer of a blessing from the priest if desired, usually goes over very well. Don't let fear of this conversation prevent you from trying this outreach. People may be welcome every day of the week, but they don't know that. Make the invitation, and make it easy for people to say, "Yes, I'll come and see."

    Pro tip: do it two weeks before you start RCIA.

68. Diversity sharing. (Basically, inviting people into cultural celebrations, with kerygma.) Our culture places a high value on diversity, and, in most ways, this is very good! We all bring different histories and gifts. We can use this interest in other cultures to highlight the ways God has worked in other cultures within our parish family. In particular, if your Anglo parish has a significant Hispanic/Latino presence, encourage them to share how different customs and traditions lead them closer to Christ. (Some examples are the Day of the Dead, Las Posadas, and Our Lady of Guadalupe.) Invite the entire town! Tell schools, language teachers, and community education organizations. Just be sure the presentation addresses how this custom or practice draws people closer to Jesus Christ.

69. Door to door survey. Door to door evangelization doesn't need to be intrusive or deep end—it all depends on how it is done. Go two or three at a time, introduce yourselves, and say you are conducting a survey on the needs of the neighborhood/town. Then thank them for their time, and leave a card inviting them to learn more about your parish.

70. Door to door, variation. Go door to door, identify yourself and say you are introducing your parish to the neighborhood. Ask for prayer requests, and follow up by sending them a letter to say that you made that prayer and that they are welcome to come to your church.

Evangelizing the Family

The family is *the* core community, and the place where children are most fruitfully evangelized and raised in the faith. Parents have more influence on their children than any other group, including teachers, peers, coaches, and social media. How do we encourage parents to share the message of Jesus Christ with their children? And how do we encourage gentle evangelization of those in our family who have fallen away, or who never had faith to begin with? The following are ways for parishes to encourage and empower families to live their baptismal call to evangelize. If you are reading this and have a family, go for it—you don't need a parish program to do most of these.

71. Teach children to pray. When you teach children to pray, you introduce them to Jesus Christ. Most Catholic parents do teach their children to pray the Our Father and Hail Mary, but children can be remarkably open to deeper contemplative prayer. Teaching them to "talk to Jesus" throughout the day is one of the biggest gifts you can give a child. Make it a habit to begin the day with blessing your children and praying with them for their concerns for the day. Check in while putting them to bed, or at dinner: How did your conversation with God go today?

72. Sharing the saints as signs of Christ. Learn about one saint a day, through an online source or a brief reading from Magnificat.[22] Saints, by definition, have conformed their lives to Christ. Ask your kids on a regular basis: How was this saint's life like Jesus's life?

73. Offer Catechesis of the Good Shepherd. This Montessori-based faith formation process focuses on drawing children to relationship with Jesus Christ through a focus on mystery and play. This is typically a parish program rather than a home-based one, although it can be adapted to home. Learn more at cgsusa.org.

74. Encouraging kids' own call to evangelize. One of the hardest things to do is to help youth be open and confident Christians in a culture that doesn't reward that. Have periodic conversations with them about how you share the message. Is it by being a good friend? By creative faith sharing? By being brave when someone challenges you?

75. Older parents: listening to fallen-away children, sharing your story. A dramatic number of older parents in our parishes live with the reality that an adult child does not practice the faith. I highly recommend Brandon Vogt's book *Return: How to Draw Your Child Back to the Church*.[23] Vogt has a thoughtful, sympathetic, and practical tone that empowers parents to handle the situation through prayer, deliberate listening, and deliberate sharing of your own faith. Parishes could use this book as a book study or as the basis of a talk or other support.

76. **Deliberate prayers in August for fallen-away family.** This idea comes from Fr. Timothy Ferguson of the Diocese of Marquette. Encourage parents or family members of those far from the faith to dedicate the month of August to prayer and fasting, through the intercession of St. Monica (feast day: August 27), the patron of parents of fallen-away children—in her case, it is was the future St. Augustine, one of the most famous theologians of the Church! Spend the month talking about it and truly dedicating prayer to it—an adoration hour, or rosaries before Sunday Mass.

77. **A kids' field day, with "parenting appreciation" support.** Create a carnival morning for kids (and make it good!), with the intention of gathering parents together for appreciation and evangelization support. Remind parents that they have a powerful vocation, ideally through their examples, and underline how they can make a difference in their children's spiritual lives. Our teens and Millennials use the phrase "I see you" to communicate support. This event could be an "I see you" moment for beleaguered parents everywhere needing a pep talk.

78. **Outreach to grandparents everywhere: do the same as above!** Grandparents have a great impact on their grandchildren, more than typically recognized. Let's honor and support the grandparents too.

Direct Service Events

These events should go without saying as essential to Christian mission, but people often are nervous about sharing the message and person of Jesus Christ within them. It's actually simple: first, we care for those in need because we are Christians, *not in order to make them Christians.* We never hold needs hostage to faith statements. *But ... we who are Christian can share who we are in the process,* and remember *whose* we are through the process. Think about your service initiatives and do a proclamation check—how do those who serve move more deeply into life in Christ? And how could those receiving care encounter the face of Christ in and through our work and friendship? There are many more options than these, but here are some to get you started.

79. **Feeding the hungry.** If your parish offers a soup kitchen, or supports one on a regular basis, what kind of spiritual support or processing should a parish provide for this work? Is prayer at the front end of it, and the back end? Could you offer a corner where people would be welcome to ask for prayer?

80. **Sheltering the homeless.** Again, if your community offers shelter to those in need, one of the quietest deep needs for these folks is being heard. Offer the gift of listening, and then offer (don't force) the gift of prayer. They can always say no. But people who know their need are likely to say yes.

81. **Caring for the environment.** This is particularly attractive to the Millennial and Gen Z generations. Cleanup, reclaim God's natural world, and share afterward: How is our environment a visible sign of invisible grace—sacramental in nature? How does nature help us draw closer to God?

82. **Free clinics, or referrals to free health care.** Free clinics are a lot of work, but worth it—the need is high. What may be simpler for a parish to offer is a process that creates referrals to doctors, dentists, and other healthcare professionals who can take a limited number of *pro bono* patients per month. Offer a relationship with those who call in need, and offer to treat "the whole person."

83. **Free haircut days.** This is a significant need … consider paying hairstylists a base rate for the day to make it happen, or hiring students from the local cosmetology school. Some may be willing to volunteer for free for a couple of hours. Make it upbeat and fun, play Christian music, and share information on joining your parish as people leave.

84. **Free afterschool tutoring for kids.** Begin with prayer, and get to know the families. What are their real needs? Do they need friends who are fighting for their kids? Do the kids need a "big brother" or "big sister"? How do you offer Jesus Christ in the context of those needs?

Learn a New "Language"

If you look at the classic missionaries from centuries past, you realize quickly they were language specialists—they learned the language of their mission field. Even the original missionaries realized quickly that there was more to communication than language. Employing a second language often means listening and adapting to the desires, insights, culture, and particular needs of the other.

A significant number of the options in this section deal with outreaches to those living with disabilities. 85–90% of those living with disabilities in the United States are unchurched—an astounding number.[24] Jesus came for everyone, but the worship, service, and other offerings may not be accessible. The best way to do an outreach is to work closely with those living with disabilities, and those who care for them. Invite those who are able into the ministry of evangelization. This is about inclusion, not charity. So what does evangelization in this language look like?

85. Regular prayer service for those with intellectual disabilities. Consider creating a prayer service (song, Scripture, preaching) dedicated to those with intellectual disabilities, but all are welcome. Advertise and let social workers, group homes, and assistance organizations know.

86. Bible study specifically for those on the autism spectrum. Include sensory dampening supports and consult with those who work with people with autism, as well as those living with autism themselves. This may be an option that is preferred in an online format: ask.

87. VBS for kids living with disabilities. Vacation Bible School is a natural evangelization week for the younger set. Create a VBS for kids living with disabilities … include fun and devotionals … invite the town. Bring in people who work with kids with disabilities (such as special education teachers at schools, direct care providers, etc.) to brainstorm what is needed and appropriate.

88. … Or adapt your VBS to make it accessible and friendly to those with disabilities.

89. **Make ASL your parish's second (or third) language.** Employ a person fluent in ASL (or learn it yourself) to translate Masses, events, small groups, and more. You could also create small group options that use chat, so the Deaf person can read, write, and participate. This is one of those situations where a person is likely to muse "no one has ever asked for ASL interpretation before." If you are in a city and you make the Mass and other activities genuinely available to this population, they will come whether they are Catholic or not.

90. **Learn the local second language.** This has nothing to do with disability, but is so obvious that it is almost embarrassing to mention it. If you live in an area with a growing population whose first language is not English, it would be worth learning their native language. It is the single most important thing you can do to reach and share with that population.

Social Media

Social media—Facebook, Instagram, Twitter, Pinterest—is simply a method of communication. It is the way people increasingly get their information, stay in casual contact, and connect with interest groups. But for social media to be a form of evangelization communication, you need to focus on *inviting and living out social media relationships*. You can take advantage of the strengths of social media via appealing presentations of the proclamation, sharing the beauty of faith in Christ in visuals and music, and taking the time to invite people to life in Christ. These can and should be part of social media evangelization work—but *every person can evangelize* simply through living their faith honestly and humbly with others online. In the end, this open life of faith is often the most powerful way to share the message.

91. **Live your spiritual life out loud.** Stop censoring your faith life online: Share your life and trust in God. Practice the virtues. Be virtuous in your language, charity, and kindness. People are watching, and they do remember.

92. **Stop treating social media friends like a special**

interest club. Be interested in others outside of your interest circle; do friendship outreach. One advantage of social media is that it can be easier to talk about deeper matters—you have time to compose your thoughts and write them out.

93. **Create a text prayer group online, with chat/text prayers.** Have you noticed Millennials and Gen Z text and chat box everything? Meet them there. Set hours where the chat room is open for shared prayer. This may require some tech savvy to set up, but you know someone who is tech savvy—ask around and this person will appear, and then ask for his or her help.

Off-the-Beaten-Track Ideas

94. **Christmastime outreach.** This deserves a booklet in itself … but basically, this is the easiest time of year to evangelize, as people look for a place to worship for Christmas. Additionally, Christmas is a difficult time for many people: they are often seeking the peace that does not come from material gifting and expectations. People want an invitation to something more. It would be worth your money to buy and send postcards to everyone in your zip code inviting them to Christmas Mass. As for the Mass itself, amplify the hospitality and deliver the proclamation within the homily. For example: the message is: "Christ came for you, in the messiness of real life, and he wants a relationship with you. He is your gift. Accept him in your heart. Your new life starts today."

95. **Create a pilgrimage.** People like a challenge, a mysterious destination, and an adventure. Pilgrimages combine all three. See if you can "create one" nearby. Now: what could that mean? Is there a church with a relic? Or a meaningful spot to get to, like a monastery? Or a spiritual event? Create a walk or bike ride to it. Bring a chaplain to walk/bike along with you. See if, on the way, you can sleep on cots on church floors. If this sounds slightly nuts, keep in mind people do this sort of communal trek; they do it without the deliberate religious motive, and afterward, they often call it a spiritual experience! (For

example, Iowa's Ride is a yearly phenomenon of hundreds biking across Iowa through one week in July.) Invite those who are spiritually curious and want a challenge.

96. **Let's go to the movies.** Show a Christian-themed movie in the local theater. Advertise, and offer free tickets to nonmembers with discussion afterward. Tugg (tugg.com) is an independent movie distributor that will show indie movies for single shows in local theaters. Many of the films are not Christian in theme, but some are. Look into it as an evangelization opportunity. Some independent Catholic film production companies are listed at #27.

97. **Free group training for a local race.** This can be as simple as a group training run every morning for a local race, and ending with a short Scriptural reflection time. I have heard of (athletic) priests reaching out to the wider community to train this way.

98. **Create a Christian life-coaching practice.** This is an interesting idea that basically takes the popularity of life-coaches and offers a Christian alternative—perhaps sounding less intense than spiritual direction, and appealing to more people who are simply curious about Christianity.

99. **Create a family camp weekend ... with the kerygma.** Camping isn't just for the youth group! What if a church created a camping weekend for families to spend time together, and enjoy bonfires with Christian songs, skits or music, devotional time, and the whole nine yards? What if families invited other families? What if each evening there was a short kerygma talk and bonfire?

100. **Science and religion talks.** Nearly all evangelization initiatives are about proposing Jesus Christ, but this one deals with a common barrier to even considering Jesus Christ. Research studies continually underline that people feel they must choose between science and religion as a worldview. Sadly, most don't realize that that faith and reason, properly understood, work in harmony with each other. This has been the Catholic point of view for cen-

turies. Any presentation, or series of presentations, that breaks down this barrier to faith would be worthwhile. Witness talks from doctors and scientists are especially helpful.

101. ***"Adoration under the Stars."*** This is an annual evangelization initiative in Kansas, where there is a night of adoration with music, you guessed it, under the stars. They have 1,300 people come with blankets and lawn chairs to a field, where they offer confession. It is deliberately ecumenical—all are invited to worship. For towns with the space, or near rural fields, this is a beautiful idea that would intrigue many to try this out. Make sure to build in a rain date.

Conclusion

Doesn't this sound exciting? Joyful? Even ... fun?

We can't allow the bad rap the word evangelization has been given to rob of us the joy of sharing the goodness of God ... or allow that bad rap to keep people in need from hearing these lifesaving words: Jesus Christ loves you, really loves you; he is real, out of mercy he died for you, and he has a remarkable plan for your life. It sounds too good to be true. But he *is* the way, the truth, and the life. Jesus Christ is absolutely, thrillingly true.

This booklet has tried to focus on the proclamation, that Jesus Christ is present to save us from our sin, our brokenness. That proclamation must be followed up by relationship—the call is to relationship with Jesus Christ through his Church. As Catholic Christians, let's not forget that we are challenged to deepen our own discipleship, and to grow in our own relationship with Jesus Christ. Part of that is intentional discipleship: prayer, sacraments, striving for virtue, living according to our call. Part of that growth involves prayerfully asking the Lord how exactly he wants us to share his Word, and bring others to encounter Jesus Christ. When people in our path respond to the proclamation with openness, let us remember to thank God for his goodness—because it is all God's work—and invite them into growing relationships within Christ's own Church. This is where Christian friendship begins. Walk with them. Accompany them. We are journeying together to the Kingdom and inviting others on the way. What a great joy the Lord has given us: we get to tell people the best news they will ever hear in their lives.

Don't be afraid; pray and take a small risk for God. The Lord does so much with the little we give him.

There is a world in need waiting to hear of God's goodness and love. Let's go!

Acknowledgments

Many thanks to Deb McManimon and Bobby Vidal for their comments on the draft manuscript, and Karen Carter for her excellent copyediting. Any flaws are my own.

P.S. Get a free "Brainstorming for Evangelization" worksheet

Do you want to use this booklet as a springboard for brainstorming what your parish can do to share the good news that Jesus Christ is for everyone? Go to gracewatch.org and click on Store > Digital Downloads for the "Brainstorming for Evangelization" handout. Use coupon code **101WAYS** to get it for free.

Endnotes

1. According to the Pew Research Center, currently 26% of American identify their religious affiliation as "none." https://www.pewforum.org/2019/10/17/in-u-s-decline-of-christianity-continues-at-rapid-pace/

2. Jonathan Merritt's *Learning to Speak God from Scratch: Why Sacred Words are Vanishing—and What We Can Do To Revive Them* (Convergent Books, 2018) is worth the read in this regard, especially the first half of the book, which statistically proves that religious language is disappearing from our culture, and describes the phenomenon of reviving dying languages—basically, by intentionally using them.

3. *Catechism of the Catholic Church*, #905.

4. Paul VI, *Evangelii Nuntiandi*, #45.

5. If you would like a handout to help you or a team at your parish do a brainstorming session, look up the "Brainstorming for Evangelization" digital download sheet at gracewatch.org.

6. The first arrow that mentions the thresholds toward intentional discipleship are from Sherry Weddell's *Forming Intentional Disciples: The Path to Knowing and Following Jesus* (Our Sunday Visitor, 2012), a book well worth reading. The second line is derived from the *General Directory of Catechesis*, #62, available from the Vatican website.

7. This idea is adapted from a process shared by Bobby Vidal, Associate Director of Evangelization for the Archdiocese of Los Angeles.

8. This is part of Saint Paul Street Evangelization's Basic Evangelization Training, and you can access this part of it through supporting Saint Paul Evangelization Institute, and accessing their School of Evangelization videos. Go to Archived Talks, Basic Evangelization Training, and the Christian Testimony tab: https://evangelizationschool.com/course/conferences.

9. "You Were Born for This" podcast, ep. 2. https://youwerebornforthis.fireside.fm/2

10. *Mark's Gospel: Onstage with Max McLean*, Vision Video, directed by Max McLean. It is available as a DVD or streaming video at https://www.amazon.com/Marks-Gospel-New-Max-McLean/dp/B003B2XP10.

11. Richard Horsley, *Hearing the Whole Story: The Politics of Plot in Mark's Gospel*. Westminster-John Knox Press, 2001.

12. Alpha and ChristLife are similar processes worth examining because they teach and embed so many evangelization skills—invitation, hospitality, praying with others, listening, sharing your story, friendship. See more at Alpha (alphausa.org) and ChristLife (christlife.org).

13. Dawn Eden Goldstein, *My Peace I Give You: Healing Sexual Wounds with the Help of the Saints*. Ave Maria Press, 2012.

14. www.heartofthefather.com

15. Damian Stayne, *Lord, Renew Your Wonders: Spiritual Gifts for Today*. Word Among Us Press, 2017, p. 107.

16. Robby Dawkins, *Do What Jesus Did: A Real-Life Field Guide To Healing The Sick, Routing Demons And Changing Lives*. Chosen Books, 2013.

17. This phrase comes from John Wimber's book, *Power Evangelization* (HarperCollins, 1986). Wimber is not Catholic, but he is the founder of the Vineyard Movement (evangelical and charismatic). However, the basics of what he proposes—that employing the gifts of the Holy Spirit in public is a powerful witness to God—is thoroughly rooted in the Gospels and the Book of Acts. In Catholic circles, it is also practiced by Encounter Ministries (encounterministries.us), Renewal Ministries (www.renewalministries.net), and the *Cor et Lumen Christi* community (www.coretlumenchristi.org).

18. https://www.nimh.nih.gov/health/statistics/any-anxiety-disorder.shtml

19. Fr. Jacques Philippe, *Searching for and Maintaining Peace*. Alba House, 2002.

20. https://www.sos-usa.org/our-impact/focus-areas/advocacy-movement-building/childrens-statistics

21. https://nationalhealthcouncil.org/wp-content/uploads/2019/12/AboutChronicDisease.pdf

22. Franciscan Media has a saint of the day online: www.franciscanmedia.org/source/saint-of-the-day; and Magnificat has some engaging short narratives on the daily saint: us.magnificat.net.

23. Brandon Vogt, *Return: How to Draw Your Child Back to the Church*. Numinous Books, 2015.

24. https://www.thebanquetnetwork.com/blog/2018/8/28/5-statistics-we-cant-ignore

www.ingramcontent.com/pod-product-compliance
Lightning Source LLC
Chambersburg PA
CBHW052128110526
44592CB00013B/1798